The Bastard and the Bishop

Also by Gerald Fleming

POETRY
One (Hanging Loose, 2016)
The Choreographer (Sixteen Rivers, 2013)
Night of Pure Breathing (Hanging Loose, 2011)
Swimmer Climbing onto Shore (Sixteen Rivers, 2005)

ESSAY
La del amor (Shadow Line, 2020)

BOOKS FOR TEACHERS
Rain, Steam, and Speed
(with Meredith Pike-Baky; Jossey-Bass/Wiley, 2005)
Prompted to Write
(with Meredith Pike-Baky; Jossey-Bass/Wiley, 2005)
Keys to Creative Writing (Allyn & Bacon, 1991)

AS EDITOR
The Collected Poetry and Prose of Lawrence Fixel
(Sixteen Rivers, 2020)

The Bastard and the Bishop

Prose Poems

Gerald Fleming

Hanging Loose Press,
Brooklyn, New York

Published by Hanging Loose Press, 231 Wyckoff Street, Brooklyn, New York 11217-2208. All rights reserved. No part of this book may be reproduced without the publisher's written permission, except for brief quotations in reviews.

www.hangingloosepress.com

Printed in the United States of America 10 9 8 7 6 5 4 3 2 1

Hanging Loose Press thanks the Literature Program of the New York State Council on the Arts for a grant in support of the publication of this book.

Cover art and interior drawing by Bruce Henderson
Book design by Nanako Inoue
Author photo by Geraldine Gibson

ISBN: 978-1-934909-70-6

In Memory of Bob Hershon

Acknowledgments

My thanks to the editors of the following journals, in which many of these poems, sometimes in earlier versions, appeared:

American Journal of Poetry: "Blue Iris," "Refugee"

California Quarterly: "Connect," "Fisherman" (as "Interview")

Catamaran: "The Old Books"

Hanging Loose: "And the Strangers Do Stay ...," "Collector of Titles," "My Andalusian Friend," "Night Scholar," "Progression," "This Water"

Hole in the Head Review: "The Black Book," "At the Visitor's Center," "Sister, they called him"

Hong Kong Review: "Nurse"

La Macchina Sognante (*The Dreaming Machine*) (Italy): "Chapel," "Club," "Island," "Name Day," "The Nightshift Brickmakers," "Over There," "Second Door," "The fire two hundred miles away," "The Weeping Man, Paris," "To My Friend Bill, in the Ethers," "To view the fireworks, then," "Winter Coat," "The tunnel foreman," "Outside Las Cruces," "Brocade Dress"

Mudlark: "At last the monochromist couldn't sustain it," "At the Lighthouse," "He wondered if his parents were too kind to him," "In Silence," "The Jokers," "Response"

New World Writing: "The Bastard and the Bishop," "*Get him out of the wind*," "*Let's organize a parade of one-legged war heroes*, the President said," "Lookout," "Persephone Off the Runway" (as "Fragment from an Interview")

Paris Atlantic (France): "In the cemetery we're between worlds ..."

Paris Lit Up (France): "Passage"

Poetry Flash: "In Recall," "The composer said that birdsong ..."

Telepoems: "*Let's organize a parade of one-legged war heroes*, the President said …" (audio recording)

West Marin Review: "The Collagist"

My thanks also to David Miller, both for his support of the project and for the words, the particulate energy informing his poems. Great thanks to Judith Serin and Ellery Akers, whose shaping of this book was essential; to Elf Diggerman; to Hanging Loose editors Robert Hershon, Mark Pawlak, Dick Lourie, and Caroline Hagood, for their faith and their work, and to Bruce Henderson for his cover painting and drawing. Finally, thanks to my wife, Gerry, who after all these years continues to abide both me and this life in poetry.

Postscript: From the outset it was my plan to dedicate this book to dear friend and Hanging Loose editor Bob Hershon, and indeed the original dedication was as such— *For Bob Hershon: 3K + 10 = 0*, the meaning of which Bob would glean: 3,000 miles distance + 10 years between us were as nothing. What was *not* foreseen was Bob's death at the cusp of winter and spring, 2021, just before this book went to press. Grievously, then, the new dedication.

CONTENTS

1. And the Strangers Do Stay

2. Passage

3. This Water

1.

And the Strangers Do Stay

Let's organize a parade of one-legged war heroes,
the President said,

fifteen years of roadside bombs, there must be thousands of 'em! We'll dress 'em in bright colors, the lost lefts we'll do red, the lost rights we'll do Air Force blue, we'll fly 'em here, put 'em up a few nights— vouchers for drinks, that's all it'll take—they'll march the half-step, we'll goose-step 'em, left flank & right, and when they're told to close ranks for the cameras, they'll look whole again in the afternoon light & our nation can forget....

Dressed in polished cotton, the soldiers came, did as they were told. Up the straight avenue they marched, young men, young women, slow but lockstep, televised, eyes raised, unwavering, arm in arm for support.

And then, as one, they fell, The Domino Effect come true, but not the way the generals had warned of it/been funded for it so long ago; there on that glorious day the one-legged warriors fell, men against women against men against men, arm in arm they went down in the clatter of prosthetics, the reds into the blues in one wave undulating down the avenue, the band on the bandstand antheming its martial pageantry of spring, cherry blossoms adrift in the April breeze.

What about one-armed men, then, said the President. *They can still salute, can't they? Let's make 'em salute. What about gurneys? Can we get guys on gurneys....*

And the Strangers Do Stay, For They Are Indefatigable

"Don't Go to Strangers" on the radio, just at the moment he was thinking of his dreams—where they'd gone, how faithful he'd been to them, which dreams still to pursue—*my time's contracting, and anyway what did they mean,* then the inevitable deconstruction of each, self-flagellation, then Etta Jones, bold, assertive on the stereo, *Build your dreams to the stars above....* live messages from dead gods.

I remember a taxicab ride at night in a downpour, she said to him once. *I thought we were on our way, but a blind man got in, needed a cab, too, sat beside me. He took my hand and said, "Don't be afraid—this dream will only last three blocks, but if you want I can stay in your mind forever," and instinctively I said, "I want."*

Chapel

They'd come upon it thirty years ago—

You were pregnant....

No—you think I wouldn't remember if I was pregnant?

Certain, though, it was the mountains of Peloponnesus, two-lane main road hardly *main*, often single lane, shrines to dead drivers along the way. The place they stopped, that's what stayed with them—a neglected chapel hardly bigger than a double bed, vaulted arches, the arches not stone but olive branches embedded in plaster, a window at the end of the nave looking out on the sea, a huge crucifix in front of the window, also olive—gnarled and gray, a Christ-figure so desiccated that for a moment they thought one of the local villagers must have willed his body to be lashed to that cross.

The chapel was stone on the outside, whitewashed, and the nave whitewashed so thinly that the wood-grain of the walls bled through. Six people and one priest would have filled the place. More shrine than chapel, a table in front of the cross, two bare wood benches serving as pews.

He and his wife were young then, and sat together that morning, alone.

They stayed twenty minutes and no one came, and soon it was apparent the place was claimed by no one, by everyone, was always open, a wayfarer's place to sit, kneel, look at the sea through the tangled cross, pray.

They continued down the road, visited a war monument, each still talking of the chapel, the way it echoed their voices almost tentatively, of the contorted Christ—*forsaken, almost human*, and then he said *Let's turn back—we can have dinner at that little town below it*, and they did, and they drank ouzo, and though they were in no need of miracle and did not ask for one, they went back to the chapel and moved the pews and spread their sleeping bags on the stone floor, and all night the cold wind came and went, and the grotesque Christ did not come alive, and halfway through the night they were cold and zipped their sleeping bags together.

He reached for her and she said *Not on your life, Buster—not with that guy looking down at us*, and in the morning they set out, wordless and content, toward Sparta.

Island

What did it mean, he wondered, that their dear friend arrived at the island not only the same day but also on the same ferry? It was he—they were sure of it—climbing into that taxi after the boat docked, the blue linen shirt he wore so often, his ragged Targus backpack. After all, this was not some offshore rock a mere seagull-flight from home: it was a thousand miles away. The husband & wife & two kids at the all-inclusive "family resort": lukewarm food & watered-down booze, pool slides for the kids, silly entertainment in a little amphitheater at night, the poolside sounds of children being chided in seven languages, those *no's* and *nein's* and *komm her's* and *venez!* and the children, indomitable, a laughter the two of them loved, *not noise to us at all—just joy*, days of it, and in the meantime their friend—whom they *hadn't heard from in six months*, somewhere on the island too?

He knew that the other man had always loved the wife, that she loved him: she brightened when he came to visit.

But she was with me the whole time.

For a day or two the husband thought he was skirting the edge of paranoia—wondered if it was just enough for his wife, by arrangement, to be within mere proximity, the Aegean encircling them, the Greek air shared.

And when months after their return the man came to visit—both of the couple happy to see him—they spoke of their trip to that island, "discovered" they were there at the same time, called it coincidence, and it was then that the husband felt the force of it between the two, understood that their talking was artifice, exercise, and they saw that he saw, and so silence for a long time: each of the three of them as if bound in a cell, and they looked at each other, intimate and grieving.

Progression

Wednesday, long day at work, off the subway, up six blocks of brownstones—his place the blue gate, he's cold, his breath steaming, stocking cap tight, keys in his hand ... locked out of his flat again.

Tenth time in a year, and not because of an affair, not because he was drunk, cruel—it's just that she's getting worse, calls a different locksmith each time—*how many possibly can be left?*—tells the story of the break-in (by now it's twelve years past, but for her it's yesterday), tells them it *was* yesterday, and again she changes the locks & though he rings & pounds & calls out to her, she cowers in her bedroom, certain The Thief has learned her name.

No longer does he go 'round the back, climb the metal stairs—it's embarrassment now, the downstairs neighbors always home—or pound or jimmy the door or break the kitchen window. It's the scene; he can't stand the scene.

So now he calls his own locksmith, waits: an hour, two; in January, fifteen degrees, it was three.

Again? the locksmith says.

Again, he says.

You're making me a rich man, the locksmith says. *Shall I keep some barrels keyed for you?*

Thank you, says the man. I'll talk to her again.

In Recall

He'd loved Jung's *Memories, Dreams, Reflections* as a young man, and if you asked him about it now he'd probably call it *enthrallment*, for what returns to him are not Jung's concepts or any particular idea, but a sense that he was being freed—certainly from the Catholic dogma he'd been yoked to for twenty years, but also sent simultaneously by Jung into a synchronicity with the woman he was falling in love with. She was discovering the collective unconscious, too, and they were unconscious together—hyper-aware of symbolism, uncovering ancient myth & metaphysics for the first time—all of this made more real as they discovered the transformative power of their bodies.

Could Jung have rung so deep a chord without the resonating vessels of their bodies? Could their bodies have felt that holiness—archetypal—without their having studied him? Did they invent those thoughts—that *heat*—simply because they were young?

In fact, they never spoke of it until this year, half a century later, when, still lovers, she said, "Do you remember when we were first dating and we were reading Jung?"

And then he:

"I remember the beauty of your shoulders."

Outside Las Cruces

My friend Peter used to tell me about how he'd sit on his front porch in New Mexico, dark days, dry days, watch lightning strike the distant chaparral—flare of burning tumbleweeds, the scrub ablaze. *Sometimes it was silent,* he said, summer thunder too far to hear or wind blowing its sound the other way, and in the distance he'd see a blade of light tear the sky/strike a patch of greasewood, flare of burning oil rising/subsiding, then the storm would move downplain, strike creosote this time, shock it, too, aflame. *I liked it best that way— silent, & I could follow it. I didn't know where it was going, but my eyes knew.*

The fires two hundred miles away,

the whole region engulfed in smoke. More than a week now, and they're assigning numbers to the air: zero to 500, and here we are at 350.

What sort of god is this? you said.

Today when we walked by the lake, the trees illumined as if in yellow streetlight, we took off our masks for a moment, put them back on. *Streetlight sun,* you said, and we gave up, went back to the car.

What god would give us intelligence but not quite enough, the keys to our destruction and a newly-lubricated lock? God of Firestorms, my love, God of Poisoned Air, God of Pogrom. Hitler his son sitting to his right, Attila to the left.

The death toll rising as in the ashes new bodies are found. It's hard to find much, they say, not a house left, much confusion there. The wood, of course, blackened, but metal melted, too, in the heat, and all the plastic, the human bodies misshapen, charred, viscous. The searchers grateful for gloves.

When the firestorm came there was no time. Fuel built over decades in the dry hills, hardwood: oak & manzanita, madrone, ceanothus, and the flares of softwood pine & fir—only one road out—then wind and a doubling of wind come of fire, embers the size of fists. The noise *like freight trains,* they always say, but this freight different, flatcars laden with trees and burning coals, and you're at the tracks, waiting to get through, and there's no getting through, just the roaring.

Ever think about what these numbers mean? you said. *Particulate matter: it's based on the density of particles in the air, the air we're breathing at this moment.*

Sure, I said. I know that.

Ever think about the particles?

Well, they're from the smoke, I said.

No: they are *the smoke. And in the smoke, the bonded molecules of what's been burned. We're breathing wood, we're breathing metal. We're breathing plaster. Fiberglass. Plastic. And we're breathing the dead. Have you thought of that? We're breathing the dead.*

They closed the schools again today, I said.

Response

He'd written a freelance political article for a major magazine—
draft after draft he'd worked on it, cutting, changing dashes to
colons and back again, then working briefly with an editor—
he was known for his style, clean copy—and the article came
out, was widely praised, called *timely*, *necessary*.

A week after it appeared the editors notified him that
they'd received a letter in response, that they'd like to run it;
they'd give him a chance to "weigh in."

The letter writer, a woman from Chicago, had taken him
to task for the imprecision of a phrase: "nothing comparable
in the least." Her complaint had to do with comparatives &
superlatives, and she'd tried to get a little gentle humor into her
letter, but then pushed it further, challenging fundamental ideas,
implying that an inability to differentiate fine comparatives
ultimately affects a writer's conclusions, "invalidating, for me,
the very *raison d'être* of the article."

The writer was embarrassed. Something about the French
affectation in her last sentence enraged him. He drafted a
response, crafted & articulate. The magazine, keen to keep
his services (they sold more copies when his name appeared
on the cover) gave him twice the column-inches as that of the
correspondent.

"Did you see my response to that letter?" he asked his wife
as she arrived home from her long subway ride, take-out food
in a thin plastic bag for their dinner.

"I saw it."

"What'd you think?"

"I saw a woman mugged at the bus stop today."

Collector of Titles

My friend won't be with us long—he knows that, I know that, and last night when I visited he wanted to give me books. Even outside the front door I could smell the cigar smoke in his study, and when I went downstairs he was in his leather chair as always, the cut-glass dish of candy beside him, those orange crescents granuled with sugar. It felt so good to be there.

"Here's one," he said. "You'll get a kick out of this. *Drink Laudanum and Live!* Someone told me Coleridge read this.

"And this one: *Car Crash Sculpture: A Survey of Interactive Accidental Art.* Think I'll last long enough to get one of those for my garden, my friend? Maybe my smashed '57 DeSoto? Think there's enough room for it out there?

"And here," he said, "take one more: *Blind Certainty in the Darkness*—isn't that just the best damned title you've ever heard? It's about an Antarctic expedition gone wrong, the leader's supposed to be charting the way, but he brings *The Collected Stevens* in his pack and gets obsessed with Stevens' 'The Snow Man,' goes a little nuts, thinks they can navigate by sound, keeps chanting, 'For the listener, who listens in the snow …' in that doleful Stevens voice …This one doesn't end well."

Then he laughed—that liquid smoker's laugh of his—and I thanked him, and kissed him on the top of the head, and took my books and left.

The Old Books

Every year the words of the poet's first book fade a little until they disintegrate on their brittle paper, go back to the native land of their language. This happens with the second book, the third …

Unanchored ink, thinks the old poet, and remembers the long-ago night with his sister, strange country, city streets, it was late, they'd been walking a long time, quiet, content, then the two of them hearing a clamor overhead, looking up, seeing a flock of geese, their wings on each downbeat caught in the lights of the city.

Club

It was their first date, and he told the woman about a suicide attempt. Not his, though—he was boastful of what he called his "cowardice" in that regard, believed that if he opposed the death penalty, that ought to include himself as well. The attempt was by his best friend in college, a terrible swimmer, who jumped from a clump of jagged rocks at Gilbert Point one winter, trying to drown himself, and was swept away. But this *swept away* wasn't what he'd wanted—within minutes the waves delivered him to a beach & he cried & drew himself up & climbed back up the rocks, his feet bloodied, dove then toward the other side but again was delivered, this time to a different beach, and now he laughed & could not stop laughing, the first time he'd laughed in a year, and he walked back to the cove and gathered up his clothes and went home.

I wonder how many of us out here are like that, the woman said.

What do you mean? the man asked.

Nothing …

I think I know what you mean, he said, *but I won't push it. And the distance between the thought of the thing and the thing itself isn't really far, is it? I'm glad he lived, for sure, but I didn't feel sorry for him.*

Well, I can tell you're not in The Club, the woman answered.

Something in her response angered him.

The Club? he said. *And its officers? President of the Vortex of Bitterness? Vice-President of Complaint Inside a Shallow Life? And I suppose all the members wear scratchy scapulars under their shirts in reverence for Our Lady of Bloodletting's Ineluctable Imminence, don't they….*

You live in a sort of prison, don't you, she said, and stood up from the table and walked away.

Blue Iris

He considered his life a tiresome journey, a dead-secret journey across water from the land of kilos & grams to that of pounds & ounces, then endless travel, odometers & pedometers, every mile logged at day's end, destination to destination—driver, taker of cabs, pedestrian. It was a vow against passion, this obsession, and it took him far over the years. *242,371 miles,* the latest entry in his diary.

The body, spectacle of accelerating decay, and ... feelings? What a word: flaccid with imprecision. As far back as he could remember they came at him: *How do you feel about that? What are your feelings on this matter?* My god, what cretins!

We would expect him to be thin and yes he was thin and his eyes sunken, his hair gone gray, his bookshelves nonfiction & philosophy, his home a plastered semicircle built against the sea.

Then the note: *Your poor daughter has died.*

And his note: *I had no daughter.*

And the next: *Yes you did, and you have another.*

There was a blue iris in the eastern field across the way. He noticed it, looked at it, and looked at the note, and looked at the note again.

Lookout

By the river, yearning for an old friend, the cab driver wonders if he's really yearning for an old friend or just yearning for an old friend by a river. Every day: pulls his cab over, gets out, stands at the rail. But this is no rustic shore: it's a kind of violence, collision of concrete & water, velocity & garbage, but still he stays there mesmerized, the engine of the old Mercedes ticking, diesel smoke drifting his way.

The old friend he imagines is no one particular. A man. *I just want to stand here,* the driver thinks, *in rain or sun, and have him come to me, put his arm on my shoulder, say,* "What the hell are you doing here looking at this stinking water? Get in the cab and go make some money. Let's meet for a beer later."

Every day at a different hour he comes here like this, every day to the stinking water.

Name Day

Afternoon party in a downtown bar to celebrate the publication of a literary magazine, most attendees younger than he, many cocktails, much shrieking, and fragments of sentences, *Subaru not a Honda I said prestigious magazine he came* on *to me Republican Neruda to the doctor on Amazon* ...

He extricated himself from the meaningless din, drove home to his country place, took a walk in the dark to clear his head, returned, went to the bathroom, stepped to the sink and noticed a chrysalis hanging from his old shaving mirror in the corner next to the window they always left open. The chrysalis was pale blue, hanging from its invisible string. He stared at it as if it were from another world, then realized that slowly over a period of months he'd been sinking into despondency. What's the metaphor here, he wondered. I shave. Transform myself. Emerge new. He pulled the mirror toward him, looked into it, *felt* somehow new—and though for these last months he'd refused to impute any meaning to anything, he became, even if temporarily, a believer in the "healing power of nature," and said *swallowtail chrysalis!* out loud, thought about the contortions of swallowing a tail, and laughed—an immoderate laugh, he thought, too wild for such a silly image.

His wife came home & said *Tomorrow's your day*, and he asked her what she meant, & she said *It's your Name Day, tomorrow is André Day, and all the Andrés in Europe celebrate it—*

But we're not in Europe, he said.

But you're still André, she said, and when she left the room he said his name again and again. *André. André.*

The tunnel foreman,

soon to retire—he'd been at it forty years—fell forward onto
the breakfast table, massive heart attack, when before work one
Friday he opened his copy of *The Seattle Times*: FORECAST SEES
NO LIGHT AT END OF TUNNEL FOR SIX YEARS.

The headline, meant to yield wry smiles, written by an
intern twenty-two years old.

All his life the man had been building arteries in the dark,
slicing veins of stone.

"You have no idea what he'd gone through," said his wife,
in a subsequent interview with the *Times*.

He wondered if his parents were too kind to him,

and when he looks back over the forty-eight-year canyon he sees mere line-drawings that he wishes could be holograms, not these sparse graphics of his father's image—his father who demanded his son call him Leonard, or of his mother, neither a drunk nor a drug addict, but a woman at the distant end of the table, long brown hair, "never heard to speak an ill word." He could hardly bring to mind the details of her face: depended on photographs to remember.

Once when he was very young he'd seen on TV that kids "ran away from home," so he announced he was doing that, and ("supportive of his independent decision") they said, "All right, son, if that's what you wish," and did not call him back as he started out the door with his grocery-bag "suitcase," did not, even for their own amusement, warn him of wolves.

When he was a teenager he'd awaken at midnight & bring his binoculars into the hills and look at the stars for hours, yearning (for what, he didn't know), sometimes falling asleep in the long grass, not returning until morning, when nothing would be said as he walked in the door. Leonard was standing in the kitchen one morning when, hair rumpled, backpack muddied, the boy came in at six. *Good morning*, said Leonard. That was it. Good morning.

Once, in high school, he'd been in a supermarket with a friend when the friend stole a bottle of suntan lotion, which upset the boy. When he told his parents about it, they listened, nodded. At the end of his narrative, when he spoke of his ambivalence—part admiration for the friend's audacity, part revulsion at the theft, Leonard said, "Good, son. No need to tell us more."

At school he'd been studying geology, and one night at dinner said to his parents, "Can we go somewhere for vacation sometime? Can we go to the Alps? There's this geologic seam that runs through the Alps that's …"

"Our town is entertaining enough, but that's an intriguing idea," he remembered the father saying, chuckling then nodding to his mother, who smiled and nodded back.

It was not as if they were rich and he was brought up by salaried others. It was not as if they were poor and his parents worked brutal jobs, long hours day after day, had no time for him. His father was a pastor, his mother the local postmaster.

And did he miss them, these almost-faceless ones, now that they were gone? Had they stolen his curiosity, his measure of adolescent anger? Lover after lover had been in his bed, and he could hardly tell one from another.

Brocade Dress

On the way back from the dance in the days of cars with bench seats, she slid over to you, put her hand on your thigh, said *Shall we park?* & she was dark & beautiful & now these many years later you see she was desperate for you & you for her & what did you say, Catholic boy? *Oh, I'd better get home* & fact was you could have said *I'd love to, but I wouldn't know what to do*—and *now* you know that that would have been OK, that she would have said *I'll teach you, then*—she was kind that way—for she'd been taught & perhaps had taught others & for her this was not new, and what a lesson it would have been.

Twenty years later you're alone on an elevator in a department store, you're going down & the door opens at a floor before the one you want & you see in the distance a gold brocade dress draped across an ornate chair & from hard right she steps into the elevator & you look at each other & you hear her quick intake of breath as she must have heard yours & she turns to face the door & at the ground floor the door opens & each of you walks away.

The Collagist

He'd hated the phrase "passed on" when he was younger, attentive lieutenant in The War Against Euphemism, railed against it once at a dinner party. But fifty years later it seemed a good fit after all, the stone wall between life & death having become curtain, curtain become membrane, membrane thinning daily as if toward some birth, some expulsion.

She was gone now, and the process of erasure & reversal had begun: the photos spread on the table and in boxes at his feet, the letters, the receipts, remainders written in her hand. *What'll they do with it anyway*, he wondered, and so into each late night it was razor-knives and scissors, one line of a letter sliced free, glued to the forehead of an old friend in a photo, the rest tossed across the room with a vigor he'd not known for years. Photos trimmed, glued to other photos. Her old horse *Bolivia*, long gone—broke loose one night, went back to her birthplace to die—now she had a rider: the drunken uncle hardly remembered, and there they go, the uncle mounted reverse on the horse, headed straight into a lake.

I could live like this for a long time, the mess of it—I'm inventing the New World—something to hold onto, something to pass on.

2
Passage

The Bastard and the Bishop

Most of the city's underground—that's how hot it's gotten up there—great descending galleries, complex, reinforced earthen walls, the temperature a steady fifty-five degrees—apartments tiered four levels down, the underground river bisecting the city, lit blue or yellow or green to denote neighborhoods, help drunken passengers on the ferry find their way home. Up there any trees left have been taken by fungus, and no mere rainstorms come anymore—just torrent, unsettled soil, foundations of shorter buildings shifting—and the taller ones leaning forward, as if peering down, as if expecting to glean some meaning from seeing old couples walking quietly, obdurate in nostalgia, on their above-ground evening *passeggiata*, the men's hands clasped behind their backs, the women a few paces behind, as if the path they trace—a script cryptic, enigmatic—would one day, by dint of repetition, translate itself into sense—a ratcheting backward into the old dimly-remembered dream of verticality, cool stone, temperate breeze.

You impute more to buildings than is there, you might say, but I say that it can't be said that buildings have no intelligence.

Memories of the old life above ground are fading, so at night they auction stories here, and the rich send their representatives to bid for them. Therefore the cellars of the rich are lined with stories, some of them my own. I don't mean stories I've invented or read; I mean stories of things that happened to me up there, things I've told out loud—the fistfight with the man slapping the prostitute on the boulevard, the drowned dog eddying in yellow light, the first time I ran for my life.

I never had the sense that these were "mine," exactly. All stories, once told, belong to all of us. But in the buying of them, the storing of them, I do feel that part of me is lost, and in fact all of us, when we try to tell our auctioned tales again, stumble on the words, cannot keep the thread.

Friends of mine often leave their homes late at night, cross neighborhoods, blue to yellow to green, find the fine houses where their stories live, then pace in front of those houses, bright light flaring from windows like hyperbole. It's as if merely being near their stories can coax them back, but I tell them it doesn't work that way. The common ones remain locked in the cellars, the sexy ones in the vaults, and the ones heavy with irony go to the poorly-lit libraries.

It's my belief that our auctioned stories speak to each other at night and are changed, exaggerated in a kind of desperation at their captivity.

There's a story I want to tell called "The Bastard and the Bishop," and it is partly about me—but if I tell it, diaphragm its sad breath into the air, and if one night, many years from now, at a fancy dinner party you hear a story called "Ten Bastards and an Archbishop at Eighty-five Degrees," say my theory is right, won't you? And remember me, think of me: I was the first of the former bishop's bastards.

At the Visitors' Center

The river came through here once, and when it left it was steam. Bad ears, that river—thought our oxbow promised *stream*, didn't know our shores so sharp they sometimes carve the consonants away. What did it expect, that river? This is a land of shattered bottles, slivered glass for sand.

You ask if all our men have artificial legs, if every door's a mirror, every woman named Conundra? There's our hotel: stay awhile, see. (What's *a while*? Time here, it's measured in vials, meted out by a five-year-old child.) And of your other questions: do all our stinging nettles sing as they sting, our wasps whisper their scent for flesh, all our birds rat-tat-tat on metal all day? Stay!

Nothing dystopic about us here, don't worry. Not a pickpocket in the place. (*So what if we have no pockets?* our Head Comedian says.) Though we live in glass houses, we have no stones. (It's true that we were prairie once, that switchgrass grew, but that was before the mountains moved in with their suitcases of white & green, the deer armed with 22s pouring out of the four-o'clock train.)

And for you today, special: we've opened our vault of secrets, for in secrets we find happiness, & there's no end to our secrets: they're like our money: we just make more.

Here's one.

Y'all have terrible taste, a tour guide shouted at us once, so to gratify his group we gathered in the public square, cut out our tongues. *What a dumb thing to do*, they said, so in chorus we said *Who's gonna give you directions out of town now, lost ones?* but it didn't sound so good, all vowel & pain, & they fled in horror, & we laughed, the old tongue-tucked-down-the-throat trick, ketchup-packet trick— that's the kind of fun we have here, we with our sharpshooting deer, sun setting through the steam of our spent river, our women's triple-callused feet strolling the strands of slivered glass, lovers spreading copper blankets for picnics.

Refugee

Jump into the river at 12:46. I'll meet you at 1. If I've got the tide tables right, the current will get you here just then. Stay close to shore. Let the river take you. Keep your head down and don't swim: to swim is to splash. Count to sixty, do that thirteen times then take the headlamp & flash it once—just once—and I'll jump in.

We can reverse this. No, rivers don't flow upstream, but we've been upstream, haven't we—and what's it gotten us? Downstream the women are more *you*, the men more me. You will like the men & the women & I will like the women & the men. No one is waiting for us, I know that; I'm not a fool. But when we've crossed to the other side, when we haul ourselves out onto a dock (surely there are docks there—so many boats plow their way upstream), when they see our faces, your body & my body will be taken into the arms of their bodies, they will say *These are people from the North, and though we are people of the South, to yet others downstream we, too, are people from the North, and would want to be taken in.* This is certain. Kindness and sweet fruit await us. The waters have not flowed red there for years. I have been told these things. I promise you: we will emerge from this green river and be made new.

In Cactus

The "leader," his thin shirt sliced by spears of yucca, six of you behind him, he with his machete, the yucca bleeding as he hacks his way through/carves a flashlit path, clear yucca-blood staining *your* shirts as you follow. You're grateful for his guidance—he in his shredded straw hat—but there's a condescension in him that you find disturbing.

This is not the kind of guide you had in mind. You'd hoped for explanatory—archaeological, historical, maybe sometimes funny—but instead, all this midsummer evening it's been silence & cactus: and now he slices his way into a clearing and says *Here is where we will camp for the night. You still have water, do you not? I should have told this to you.*

You should have known to bring more water. You'd first met at the hotel lobby, the group of you, cocktails in hand, he'd walked in promising adventure, an ad-hoc overnight in which *if things went very good* you'd see *the constellations so big they are out there,* he'd *take care of all 'rangements* (he meant *arrangements,* you're sure, but you never asked him to define them), and now here you are, cold setting in ("A desert gets cold at night," you hear the elder local woman in your group say—she, who you think never should have come this far), the clearing inside the ring of cactus just adequate for the seven of you to lie down on the plastic drop-cloths he's spread on the rubbled soil, rocks piercing the plastic, and now he distributes airline blankets, *One each now,* he says. *That is all in my believing you will need.*

And he's not staying! He's not staying! *I must now leave you for a time. I have business of family....* Now suddenly shifts to his native language, the old woman translating ... *If I am not back by morning, I will bring food when I do come.* Then back to English: *Now: is there anyone who has not water ...* and a few of you nod, and he shrugs his shoulders, says *Share, then, I am sure,* and is gone.

You settle in under your airline blanket, sharp rocks finding your back, remember the last line of the novel you'd just that morning finished: "Two of us were left then, still certain he would come...."

Passage

One night I thought I was floating in it, she said—*so many men I was sure a milk-white river was inside me, men inside, men outside, naked and fat and white, and all I could do with my body was to float until the night was over, until I reached another shore.*

The next morning on an impulse I struck him flat on the face and for some reason he did not strike me back. I am human, *I said, but he said You are shit and your dialect is shit and I will tell you when you are human. I will tell you when your debt is paid.*

When they brought us here I saw a girl with a chair strapped to her back. What is that, *I said, why is* that.

She is being trained, he said. When she arrived she was wild, she was a flock of crows attacking the eagle's nest. But she knows better now—she knows better, and soon you will, too.

Persephone Off the Runway

After the fracture her leg withered. I was sent to interview her about it. I remember it in black & white, somehow—she, propped sideways in a leather chair, her good leg thrust over it, her bad leg tucked under at a slant. I had on a white shirt & black pants, black shoes, and sat in an aluminum chair, glass of water in my right hand, pen in my left, notebook on my knee.

I was sent to ask about the accident and her modeling career, the concept of *runway*, which was hers no more, an irony in the word now—I was to bring out that irony for a headline. Young then, moon-faced; in retrospect I see that I was set up, ignorant of her reputation.

I started in and she just shook her head.

Icarus, I thought she said, and I thought, O.K., I can go with this, fall from a great height, unthinking …

I can see a similarity there, I said, *but say more, please. Icarus flew too close to the sun—he was warned, as your agent warned you not to go to Istanbul?*

No, she said. *Not that Icarus. Ichorous*, and she spelled it: *I-C-H-O-R-O-U-S. Know what it means?*

I admit I don't.

Having the quality of a watery, bloody discharge—usually from a wound. From ichor. *But do you know what* ichor *used to mean? A fluid, a heavenly fluid—running through the Greek gods' veins. Vanity Fair compared me to Persephone once, the way I'd disappear part of the year, and it sort of caught on, and for a while that dispensation served me. But you know, strange thing. Ever have a horsefly loose in your house—came in through the open window—can't find its way out? Can you bring that sound to mind? Every time someone called me Persephone I'd hear that fly, that shit-fly, there in the background, as if the sound itself was some portent, some preface to the accident. And here I am, forever in the fucking underworld, and you have stepped into it, my friend. Want to meet Hades? He's in the other room. Come over here, sit right down next to me. We'll give you an interview. Okay: let's go. Ever been in a Turkish hospital?*

To view the fireworks, then,

she tied me to the oak at the top of the hill. She'd been nervous to go there alone, and knew I hated fireworks. I tried, I really did, to think of their origins—invention, possibility, transformation—tried to respect their carbon, their barium, phosphorous, calcium, but then I got lost in gunpowder, its ultimate effect surely imaginable to the early Chinese inventors.

And the spectators down there—some vague sense of optimism, I guessed, represented in those starbursts, the whole abecedarium: aerial, barrage, bombette, bottle rocket, brocade, comet, cone, confetti, all the way to sky rocket, wheel, whirlwind & whistle....

And the things scared me, I admit. But for this one night— *once only*, I agreed to play Odysseus tethered to the mast.

Isn't the sky spectacular enough, I asked, *aren't starbursts in our own heads when we're angry quite enough? And the crass ambition of it—this one higher, that one bluer, louder... And the goddamn whistling, anyway: do they need to whistle, too?*

The fireworks that night, distant, were being shot from a barge in the bay, a costly enterprise in a time when people in the districts they flared above were hungry. Nonetheless, the city fathers thought them necessary, Beacons of Hope.

Fuck beacons, fuck hope, I said, straining at my ropes as the first Silver Salute went off.

Can you just shut up and let me have my moment, she said.

How long does a moment last, I said—*does it continue through crossettes, through comets?*

I don't know, she said. Do you remember the time your truck broke down in pouring rain out on Skyline & you called & asked me to come get you? Do you remember you insisted we name our daughter Tiara and I argued & argued but then agreed? Do you remember the time ...

OK, OK, I said. *Bring on the missiles, bring on the mortars. I'm your prisoner here*, and watched the exploding lights, sure they were falling toward me.

Get him out of the wind,

one of them said, and that seemed strange—the voice that said it, *one of them*, becoming human that moment, as if there could be a chance that not all hope was lost. But of course hope *was* lost—there were just minutes now, and, facing the wall, away from the wind, the withered body itself seemed something to be cared for, grateful it wasn't *in* wind—that northeast blade of ice that had insulted it for thirty years! So yes, in the last moments there it was: kindness in a human voice and the gratitude of a body still alive, and it was *his* body, and though he knew the end would be quick, and though he could not know how painful, and though of course there was fear and it was rising, something inside him rejoiced.

Over There

Strange how even beyond The Great War *Over There* has meant so many things to so many men—not exactly a euphemism, more an avoidance to name the geography where a particular slaughter occurred.

When he was Over There he woke each day and saw himself as feudal, loyal, in the employ of some dumb Lord, but now he was Back Here, and the fact that he was able to *shower* seemed impossibly luxurious, a gift against a remembered air that was all grit all the time, and so he rose earlier than the others, showered before the heat of the day would render its effect useless, and he'd dress—for battle? for no battle? *We never know, we underlings. But my body's ceremonially clean, well clad, flak jacket cinched tight.*

He liked the word *clad.* That was the knight part, and if he could hold that notion quiet within him, close to bone, share it with no one Back Here—then, if *something happened*, he would be there for it, trained now—not a stand-in for the pitiful man who went so thoughtlessly Over There.

Shot

A jagged trapezoid of apartment buildings in an old city—six stories high, the buildings all stone, the walls of each apartment stone, the floors stone, the little central courtyard cobbled, a few emaciated trees.

4:15 on an August morning, the time of deepest dark, hot night, many windows open, the windows single-paned, wooden-framed, no breeze ruffling anyone's curtains, the heat—not unusual in the old city—oppressive.

No noise from the street, no car nor drunken voice, and a shot rings out. No sound precedes the shot, no sound follows. The shot is not from the street. It is from within an apartment. No single shout before the shot, no prelude of rising anger, no single syllable, no sound after.

1.
Many in the complex are awake: unable to sleep, hot summer night, some reprising old mistakes, some luxuriating in erotic scenes, some hearing again their own words they wish they could uninflect, wish be taken back.

2.
A woman, well into her seventies, hears the shot; a few seconds pass, and she begins to weep, staring upward into the dark, her weeping not heavy, almost silent—her breath controlled. Here in this poem we can be near her, but she would not want us near her.

3.
A man on the first floor has lived in the complex forty years. He is awake, an expert in nightsound—the slowly passing cars outside the gate, the echo of wine bottles tossed into the blue bin, the sounds of lovemaking in all its variations (he enjoys that greatly, and it is cruel to him), drunks fumbling with rings of keys in the courtyard, the artificial mirth of parties gone too late—weariness in the laughter— and the deep silence between 3 and half-past 4.

The shot occurs into silence, through silence, and the man gets up from his bed, turns on a lamp, goes to a small metal safe bolted onto a bookshelf, spins the dial, opens the safe, picks up a gold ring, looks at it, puts it back into the safe, closes the door.

4.

This is a city with a history of wars, and because of what happened in those wars, when people in this city hear a shot, near or far, they do not lean out of their windows nor call out in question. If they are in bed with someone and they hear a shot and the other person is sleeping, they will not wake her, might not even mention it in the morning.

But the shot stays with them.

5.

(How innocent the air was before the shot! And after, a purple tone, as if bruised.)

6.

In one of the apartments a young boy in Batman pajamas half-hears the shot, stirs a bit in his sleep, turns over. He dreams of his mother calling him home from the courtyard.

7.

And those who hear the shot—insomniac or briefly awake or gliding into sleep & wakened—each encounters their moment of denial—a flat clothbound book falling to the floor from a high shelf, a door slammed shut by wind, a branch of hardwood snapped, a box tossed through the gate—each image eliminated, then a reckoning, and a tender thought toward self: that one could have hoped for such a simple thing.

It is the silence after the shot that unnerves them. In retrospect they admit they'd hoped for laughter. Even, they are ashamed to admit, for sirens—distant, then closing in.

Second Door

Shanty dwellings dwarfed by trees, first scene of his son's film, black & white, the shanties only partly roofed, their skip-sheathing exposed, clapboard siding slapped up with so few nails that it slumps uniformly to the right, the corner of each house decomposing, holes through which wind & rats can move freely—and the trees, eucalyptus planted once as windbreak, lower branches gone, their fallen bark bent in half-circles on the ground, upper branches dry, as if the least wind would send them crashing down.

Over and over the father watches this scene, the lone figure in black emerging from one door, carrying a hatchet, entering another in a similar building, smoke rising from the chimney inside that second door.

The father had been grieving his own stupidity, bad investments, rash loves, absence, stubbornness. He phones his son once in a while, gets no answer.

The film is out in the theaters, the father pays his money and over and over to watch the scene, smoke rising & rising from that second chimney, the man bent as he is bent now, the man entering that second door.

Sister, they called him,

& it's too complicated to get into here: let's just say it had to do with this family of eighteen (five parents, Wyoming), the Sixties, shared clothes, few shoes, one bureau of drawers to serve thirteen kids less than nine months apart, competition (frantic hands in those drawers), five parents in the stone-strewn field all day, field that yielded nothing—desiccated carrots, cabbages like cardboard—those same parents giving each child a legal name (after #7, though, papers filled out, never turned in, "6.5" they called the one buried near the failed kale, "not notated," the father decreed, "no need—should have fed it to the others") (no laughter from the women) and Sister, not quite the youngest (not clear who *was* the youngest), *him* not ever informed what underwear to wear, what shirts (if any were left), & anyway this was just about the time the parents, Our Parents, they called them (though one of the kids, an older girl, once joked that Father-parent should be called Faster Get It Over, that's what the Mother-parents called him up there in the room), but only a few knew it was a joke & the boy didn't, that's for sure, & anyway his Random Clothes Period (lasted nine years) was around the time the Parents stopped calling them any names at all, just hollered Brother or Sister (*Suster*, one of the mothers pronounced it) and because of what he often ended up wearing they called *him* Sister, but there was one girl, the one who joked the Faster Get It Over thing, who whispered to him one day, *You're not Sister, Sister: you're Brother, and don't forget that*, but that one, she walked out of the house the night Father-parent said *Come upstairs, I want to teach you fealty* & she went upstairs & learned *fealty* and then just before the sun came up Sister sat up in the middle of the floor-blankets & snorers & saw her go to the drawers, pull out some things & not put on shoes but *carry* shoes & she was gone, Sister never saw her again—& I'm sorry, I just can't get into all the history of the Sister thing & why he kept that name even after the Authorities came in their blue vans & by the time Sister was in the group home, by the time he was as old as the girl who left, they said *We want to give you a name, what about Cody, what about Cheyenne, what about Orrin*, but *Sister*, he kept saying, *Sister*, so they gave him Sister, & of course that part's just part of it, not the Before Part about the Father-horsewhip or the Mother-shotgun (them taking turns & all that) & the Father-accident & sirens & the other Authorities, so Sister he goes out into the world, finds Our Lord Jesus Christ & meets a priest who says *You have a vocation and we're sending you to a special place*, and Sister thinks he'd said *vacation* & anyway likes it where they send him, he has his own room & soon they call him Father Sister, *and that's where the trouble started*, they say, it had to do with a *certain sermon*, one that went south they say on the *Immaculate Conception*—but that part, that's a really confusing story....

At last the monochromist couldn't sustain it—

all that gray, all that black, that endless white! Gray hoods, black pants, white shoes, black police cars striped with white, asphalt roofs, ebony violins strung with tail-hairs of old gray mares, black fedoras, black tea, squid-inked noodles, whitewashed rooms backlit with black lights, each jail cell black-barred/gray-bunked, brands of black wine drunk at every sad feast... and coffins, of course: black dirt thrown on those steel-gray lids.

Black Sunday, Black Monday, every disease black plague.

White people who hardly saw the sun—skin so white it became a precept that even within the confines of their dark bedrooms a white man and wife may not expose more than a flash of teeth, no more flesh than a face-worth, lest it blind.

Then one day it happened—the supply of stain, no longer available. Then the supply of dye. Then the tea, then the extinction of ebony & the overfishing of squid, gone the ingredients of asphalt, the industrial mixers of white & black to gray—all of this remediable, they told themselves, and though the President-for-Life forestalled panic across the land—*Go back to your homes*, he said, *we'll have the black back soon, the white, all the gray you'll need for days*—panic was imminent.

And of course we can fill it in. Years pass, nothing done, the old garments fading, tattered, hardly worth wearing, the asphalt rutted, blanched weeds poking through, the roofs decayed, the walls' black pigments flaking, and this was no new Great Awakening, no Miraculous Averaging, this was just something that Time does—there in her orchestra seat, twelfth row back, sketchpad in her lap.

Pass the pastels, she says to her assistant.

The assistant, sleek bronze skin half-lit in the stage lights, yellow cowboy hat, legs crossed, blue jeans, toenails painted red, touches Time's knee, slides her the big box of pastels.

Let's see how this goes.

The Listening Room
—after Magritte, for Dick Lourie

One does not come here to wear headphones. They're considered unholy—obscene, even. And you'd think there'd be carpet, acoustic ceiling tiles, sound-walls, woofers, tweeters all around. No: the door closes tightly, locks behind you (you did, after all, sign the beginner's one-hour contract), the bare floor gleams, the wooden chair comfortable but uncushioned, your feet fit the floor just right, and … a simple apple.

At first you don't understand. You've come here to listen—*a transcendent experience*, they say, and you're locked in now, afternoon light fading from the single window, a minuscule table, an apple on that table that in its isolation seems to grow by the moment.

Whose is this voice? It is your own, you recognize it, but its tone deeper, its words serious, as if sulfured. *You wanted Mahler*, it says, the voice coming directly from the apple, the apple itself surely an optical illusion—seeming to swell, the table diminishing.…

You pick up the apple. It expands in your hands. Turn it. *No wires!* Press its skin: hear the click made by your thumb: your old trick to know a ready apple.

It breathes. You can hear it. Surely someone's installed electronics! You turn it over in your hands, it's getting heavier, you smell it: apple. You're becoming agitated, mouth-breathing, your breath quickening, the intake of your breath like wind over mountains, the outflow wheezy, braying of distant donkeys. And now your heart beating—they don't call them eardrums for nothing—and the tinnitus you've lived with for years— those twin violins—and now castanets of vertebrae in the neck.

You wanted Mahler, didn't you, the apple says again, voice slowed half-speed this time, lugubrious, the apple nearly the size of the room now.

An apple is meant to be eaten! You bite in: apple. Bite again: apple, its skin tough, your chewing precisely the sound your arms make when swimming in rough water, rhythmic like that, storm coming in, you're making fast for the shore, Sicily, Bay of Taormina, 2003, your wife waving from her yellow lounge chair, calling you back.

But there must be something at the core! You rip it apart with hands/arms/elbows, find not a single transistor/capacitor, the apple in fleshed chunks all over the floor—and the table—gone—had you imagined it?—now seeds and more seeds, no dead Mahler there, no Alma—gust of wind, the door swings open, the hour's over, proprietor comes in:

It's just apple. Apple all the way. Don't you remember?

The Black Book

Each Sunday he does this: wide-nibbed #3 Permanent pen, starts at the edges—sure hand, careful rectangles, works his way in, the sheets of paper blacken, the white space contracting with each stroke, obscuring permanently what he wrote the week before. Yesterday, his poem: *September, calm waters / warp of mirror-light / the solitary fisherman / twenty-two days at sea / bends / sees his own kind face …* lines disappearing now in the black ink, the air heavy with fumes of it, first one pass: *September, calm / warp of mirror / the solitary / twenty-two days / bends …* the poem's sense lost now as the old space filigreed with words drowns in ink, soon the whole script gone, fish & fisherman, warp & mirror—bound to heavier black, the page put away now, added to the rest, then at year's end the whole sheaf of it covered in goatskin, sewn, its red-inked cover (picture of a schooner, drawn by a friend) sent into the dark, too, and now it's all black, the black bleed on the back of pages *like bruises*, someone said, and he calls it—as he always calls it—*The Black Book*.

New Year's Eve he has a party at his place, his friends drink to the new Black Book, take turns holding it—see if they can find a word or two (they rarely do). They like holding it, but at last they pass it forward, give it up, gather at the woodstove, watch him toss it in.

Grand Design

His hands gripping the pulpit, the reverend proposed a prayer.

"Lord, humble us before thee."

Hear our prayer, the congregants murmured.

"Let us be a mere molecule of oxygen in the great sky of your Being."

Hear our prayer.

"When we are under the illusion that our lives are stable, let us recall the avalanche of 1499 that buried 400 mercenary soldiers at St. Bernard Pass in Switzerland, for we are your mercenaries, Lord, and never can know your desires for us."

Hear our prayer.

"When we believe the Richter scales of our lives are at zero, show us our arrogance, Lord, and let us bring to mind Tokyo and Yokohama, 1923, where the 8.2 corrective force of your goodness brought 143,000 souls back into your arms.

"When we are basking in what we perceive to be the warmth of your dispensation let us bring to mind the Coconut Grove night club fire, Boston, 1942, wherein 491 sinners were removed from this world of perdition.

"We are immigrants to the country of your kindness, Lord, but if our hearts are not pure, you surely apprise us of it, as we remember 1874, November, when you set alight the immigrant vessel *Cospatrick* off the Cape of Good Hope, your humor not lost on us there...."

Hear our prayer, said the parishioners, and began looking at each other.

"When we are in the metaphorical produce aisles of the world, fingering disdainfully the fruits and vegetables you so graciously grant us, let us remember ants, Lord—black ants that rose from the earth in great battalions, devoured every vegetable in Kach, India, 1791, its heathen residents sinfully resentful, calling Kach a God-forsaken place, *ants*, Lord, for we remember them and remain aware that they are your servants, too, and nothing truly is God-forsaken...."

The pastor left the pulpit, sank to his knees in the sanctuary.

"And when we are on our death-beds, Lord, being force-fed, let us remember your famines and exult: Northern China, 1878, India, 1899, and when we are drooling from the sides of our mouths let us praise you and remember decades of drought, and when heaving in fever let us recall the Great Sweating Sickness of 1506—London—death within three hours—and when we are gasping our last breaths let us recognize that you've *given* us those breaths, and recall the ingratitude of decades of buried miners, Manchuria, 1931, Rhodesia, 1972—for Lord, your smitings are various and wondrous, the Sunderland stampede, 1883, cannibalism in Ireland, 1886, Bulgarian-Greek wars, Seventh Crusades, Siege of Vienna, great winds you've exalted to the Fifth Category, you've a plan for us, Lord, you are there for us, even from that universal distance you are everywhere, in your Grand Design we implore you, look with favor on us now through the windows of the flaming children's hospitals...."

Hear our prayer, Lord, he said, *Oh, hear our prayer*, on his hands and knees now, his voice muffled in the carpet, his congregants gathering quietly around him.

3
This Water

The Jokers

"So I told you, Frank, I never trust anybody I can't tell a joke to—especially a bad joke," the bartender said. "So yesterday I say to my boss, 'Did you hear about the gardener's impatient wife? She pre-seeded him in death,'" I say.

"'What?' the boss says.

"'She pre-*seeded* him in death,' I say, and he says, 'That's *not* funny. My father was a gardener and my mother died first,' and it came to me then that jokes are really just a way of talking to each other about death, don't you think?"

I told him no, I think they're a way of saying *fuck off* to time.

"Isn't that the same thing?" he said, and I said, "Sure, I guess you're right," but I didn't see it at the moment, really, and in a way I lied, and thought a little, then wondered if lying, too, was a way of buying time....

And then he said, "How's this one: two roosters, two randy roosters, perched on a stone wall. One says to the other, 'A cockatoo will do....'"

I laughed, thought it was a great joke, and he said, "You know, you're one of my most trusted friends."

"You can't be serious," I said.

My Andalusian friend,

by day a security guard & lunch-break scholar of French history, by night a mad Flamenco guitarist, used to tell a story about the recluse Proust and Picasso and a clarinet. Proust, he claimed, was a virtuoso clarinetist, performing Beethoven sonatas on his pristine *Barbier*. He'd been told he must meet *this Picasso*, so invited the painter up for tea and madeleines. Picasso arrived late, not keen on the idea of tea, preferring wine. A bottle of Château Haut-Brion and a plate of olives were brought; a butler poured half a glass, Picasso took the bottle from his hand, filled the glass to the brim.

"Mr. Picasso," my friend told me Proust said. "I entertain few guests, but to each I put a different test."

As he said that, the butler entered with a silver tray and Proust smiled widely, all five parts of his clarinet arranged on the tray, now set beside Picasso's Haut-Brion.

"They say we are equal geniuses in our respective arts, Mr. Picasso. I believe that artists must know the other arts as well. Would you be so kind as to put my clarinet together so that I might play for you?"

Picasso took a drink of his wine, picked up the lower joint, jammed it on top of the upper joint, tossed it to the side of the table, dropped the barrel into his glass of wine, brutally conjoined the mouthpiece with the bell, stuffed an olive into the bell, blew the thing like a toy horn—the olive rocketing into Proust's napkined lap—stood up, and left.

I've looked for this story everywhere. No corroboration. I've found stories about Proust frosting Joyce, Proust following short-haired Colette around a party calling "Hermes! Hermes!" & laughing madly, nothing about any clarinet.

I haven't seen my friend in years. The last time he wrote he claimed he'd been skippering a yacht headed toward New Zealand, had engine trouble, drifted two weeks before the Australian navy helicoptered spare parts to him, that he'd traded his guitar to a woman "of unequaled charms" in the

Cook Islands for "lessons in the realm of tactility," that on her last night with him she'd picked up the guitar and played Britten's "Gloria" by heart, "And oh, by the way," he wrote, "that Proust story—not sure of its veracity—I'm thinking now it might have been Dali & Braque, and not a clarinet but a telescope. Braque was an amateur astronomer, you know...."

The Sentimentalist

He came across one of his old letters. Why he kept it, he didn't know: fifty years, now—*almost parchment, for god's sake!*—brittle in the oak filing cabinet, taken out now on this winter afternoon degenerated into nostalgia, sadness not of life gone wrong but of life loved & soon to be left: this from his trip to the *South Seas*, they called them then—a photo in there, that ridiculous striped cardigan he wore, and torn corduroy shorts—was it shamelessness or poverty?—*proud poverty*, he thought: food enough, adequate shelter, barely enough money—he'd worked his way to Australia on a student ship, two-to-one ratio women to men, but that was as nothing to him: he was in love with her, a first love that would last through the decades, his letter from Melbourne beginning *I see young people in Bourke Street playing and think of you....*

When he read this the intervening years, too, became as nothing: there he was on Bourke, two cellists and a violinist playing a Jobim song, the singer a beautiful young woman, cascading hair: "Sem Voce," he remembers it was, slow, and what came back most strongly was his standing there & staring: sensing he was not in Melbourne but home, understanding that his life had changed forever, that his body had been possessed by this woman at home, altered permanently, a kind of abduction, that a new tenderness lived inside it, that the sentimentality he'd always scoffed at held something authentic now, as if he'd been given membership in humanity by way of the love of this woman so unsure of herself at the time.

And here he was years later, maudlin in the privacy of his studio. *Stop it!* he thought—some of the "Sem Voce" lyrics now drifting through his brain—it was an I-Can't-Live-Without-You song, a Love-Never-Be-Far song, a Suffer song, it was all too much for him, his wife gone, rain steady this afternoon, a heavier storm due tomorrow, *My god, I've become a slavering old man! Good Christ almighty! Person from Porlock, knock on my goddamn door!*

Winter Coat

It was only because you needed that winter coat that the cat, shut inside one of your trunks, was able to live. Of course the coat was fouled, the cat a mere suggestion of cat, your grief that he'd run away now replaced by self-loathing. But you nursed him back: day by day he gained weight, the bare patches grew fur, his own winter coat glowed, his eyes regained their focus, and soon he was able to jump from floor to window ledge again.

It was then, of course, that he left, and that you began, season after season, to walk the streets in that dry-cleaned coat, calling his name.

To My Friend Bill, in the Ethers

Lines from your writing come back to me. Melancholy accordion on the radio (Piazzolla, "Milonga del Angel,"), then guitar-runs in homage to Django, I'm staring into the distance on this road I've driven so many times between home and the too-expensive grocery store, and lines of yours come in: *the ceremony eats my strength / drinks I've drunk come on …* the weight of them, the cost of them, which I among few knew. Caught in the same stupidities—our loyal & loathed companions down the jagged decades—I think of that great last line of your monkey poem—miniature *bête noir* who in the poem you kill & kill again, at last banish far into the past & you're at a bar & there he appears, close beside you, *Where're we goin' tonight?*

    Miss you, Bill. Wish you were here.

In Silence

The strength of her silences sometimes frightened him. Most of his were temporary, had questions implicit in them, and if a companion were perceptive, he or she would allow that silence its time, then ask the buried questions.

Sometimes his own questions to her were a challenge—what *he* would have hoped to have been asked—*Is that what you really mean, or is it more than that?*—or sometimes they were just fillers against the void—*What do you have in mind for dinner?*

So in a sense, there never really was silence with him: only incipience, a mute hesitance more pause than silence, a window-shade drawn on a tightly-wound spring.

Hers, though, held a solidity, a sense that there'd been no time before or after, and though Zen masters might have deemed it "centered," it was not that—its time was neither circular nor linear: time itself puddled in front of it, useless measure ticking its hours.

Was it *productive*? Was it *calming*? Did it serve to *deepen*, was it *idle, hostile*?

None of these things. It was as if she were a diamond setter by day and by night she worked to tweeze the diamonds out.

And it was the draw-string velvet bag of her diamonds, he knew, that he kept in his pocket, fuel cells for his movements, for his nerves, for his own silence, rarely inquired-about by her, and thus rarely answered.

The nightshift brickmakers listen to
Beethoven on their lunch break—

it's deep winter, three pallets are in, the first kiln in the row of immense kilns fully fired, the noise of its gas jets audible even beyond the thick firebrick, and in the red brick lunchroom the men eat their sandwiches, "Ode to Joy" blasting through the speakers one of them brought in, the Beethoven too loud to allow small talk, the bread in the sandwiches delicious, a full moon rising through trees in the long window behind them.

Nurse

He gets out of bed. That is, his nurse gets him out of bed and sits him up and arm-by-arm leg-by-leg dresses him, and today is Tuesday, no-shaving day, and the nurse is glad of that but he is not glad of that, for he misses the warm water, the white shaving cream, and the sight of her hands on his face in the mirror, so gentle, always so gentle.

And now she brings him to the kitchen, puts oatmeal into his mouth and wipes it from the sides and places into his mouth the straw for the fruit juice and he sucks at it, loses some of it, she expects that, sponges it, and now slowly spins his chair around, finds his scarf, his hat, stands him against the sink & puts his jacket on, says *Can you stay there?* and he cannot quickly answer but can nod, so nods, and she gets his chair and settles him back into it, wheels him out the door on this warm November day, and they head down rue d'Assas toward the Luxembourg Gardens.

She does not speak in the four blocks there, and neither does he. She wheels him down the gravel ramp and finds a place beside the rectangle of grass in front of the Senate, sun low in the sky but still warm, hothouse dahlias in bloom at the edge of the low iron rail.

Now she pulls up a metal chair beside him; he can hardly move his head, his black hat casts a shadow across his face, his lower lip is wet, and she takes out a glossy magazine and begins reading to him.

The nurse is a young woman, a third his age. She might be from his country, she might not. Her hair is dark & long, bound at the back with a simple bamboo stick. She wears frilled leather boots, yellow and black. Her skin is lustrous black.

She is reading aloud what must be a story, and she's a good reader, an emphatic reader, and though they're in a public place and many people pass on the gravel path behind them, she doesn't care—she reads the dialogue in varying voices, and it's clear he's listening, for he laughs once in a while a nearly inaudible laugh, minimally convulsive, leaning forward, a slight smile on his face, and she continues reading as he stares off across the garden to the distant trees and Montparnasse Tower, soon slumps a little forward, testing the straps that hold him, falls asleep.

An English-speaking couple passes behind them.

"Not for me," the man says. "Pull the plug. *Agony in the garden.*"

The nurse, multilingual, hears this, turns her head and watches them as they walk away.

Connect

In his isolation he heard the neighbors' pounding and the kids' calling out from the courtyard as signals: no matter that the pounding was from a woman two floors down hanging a photograph of her father—three freshly-caught trout in his right hand—the woman remembering the night he brought them into the house, gutted them in the kitchen sink, wrapped them in foil, baked them in butter & garlic—how happily, without conversation, the family ate. No matter that the boy in the courtyard was calling up to his good friend, who responded from the sixth floor with their special whistle that meant *My dad's home—I can't leave—don't come up....*

His was a singular affliction. He read all day, did not go to work, and his days were lost into other days: on Monday this week it was Oppenheimer, Tuesday Rimbaud, Wednesday and Thursday consecutive Dinesen, and soon he was so immersed in his biographies that he forgot who *he* was, wondered that he'd ever cared, and welcomed into his world that day the five blows of the hammer, for they signaled the hour he'd cook dinner, and the boy's voice rising past him, *Jean-Paul!* as his signal to start Sartre.

In the cemetery we're between worlds and speak of Kafka's Josef K.—

Watch out for fresh mounds of dirt, you say, and the day darkens but not entirely, and a light fog comes in, and as we weave among the rows we speak of the six joined rectangles of rotting wood under each stone then go quiet, walk a long time pausing at each name and at last you say, almost as if in prayer, *This feeling we have—it's not fear, it's just that each grave is a page— it's as if we're making our way through the book, displacing secrets scribbled in the margins of the text. We take our steps for granted, but each insults the dead.*

At the Lighthouse

He saw her turn over in sleep, and though he couldn't count the times he'd seen her do that, the way she did it this time was not comfort but barrier, not soft shoulder but steel wall. One day she'll soften, he thought, but I have work to do.

Was it last year they'd climbed around the ruins of the old lighthouse? Great circle of rubble, the stones horse-drayed to that remote granite peninsula two hundred years ago, the rock not native, but a kind of fieldstone. But it wasn't the stones that failed: it was the mortar—too much beach sand, too little lime, salt in the water.

The foundation was just the right height for sitting on, so they sat & ate their lunch there—she at twelve o'clock in the circle, he at three.

They claim this is the foggiest place on earth, she said, and when she said it she was in the clear, her black hair blown sideways. He looked down at his sandwich to take a bite, and when he looked up again she was lost in the fog, the rest of her words trailing off.

Are you still there? he asked, but she couldn't hear him. He could no longer see her, and now his feet, his legs, his hands disappeared, the fog pouring and pouring down.

Fisherman

"I'm an amateur," he said. "I write, rewrite, then night comes
'round, I stand, turn on the light, switch on the heat, head to
the kitchen, cook, sit down & eat. That's what I do with my
day. Not that glamorous!"

He said that to me once, but he's no amateur. In the waters
of our language he owns his own sea: poised there at the edge
of his separate shore he casts, tracks the leader, waits—quick
shock through the tips of his fingers, reels in: the ratcheting
click, rise of scales & iridescent skin, sound after sound bound
into his work, and now this new note finds its way in.

He was the kind of man who invited everyone he met to his house,

and because he worked as a baseball scout he traveled the country, met athletes, coaches, their wives & children, strangers in bars. He was garrulous. He was loud.

How can a man shake hands with so many in a day? He'd conquer whole continents if war were waged with clasped hands.

Some did come stay at his home. He lived in a remote place so that guests would need to stay the night.

They'd arrive mid-day, he'd take them on a walk down the dirt road into town, they'd buy something at the amazingly inexpensive antique store, then back to the house for drinks & dinner, wine & more wine, but they didn't know that his own gin was water, his red wine diluted, and they'd be charmed by his attentiveness as he listened to their stories, *Tell me more*, he'd say, *I can't get enough of this*, and of course they would tell him more, and he'd nod, but there was no reciprocation, and of course, as the night crept on, the dark stuff would come out, it always came out, and he'd soak up that dark until he reached what in his own mind he called *the obscenity point*—he loved reaching the obscenity point, loved mining it—and soon he'd say goodnight, then, in the morning, shrug off the obligatory apologies and send them on their way with their antiques.

"I feel drained," some would say in the car.

"You drank quite a bit. We all drank quite a bit."

Night Scholar

The scholar was blocked, tempted to plagiarism for her dissertation, but afraid of being found out—easy, these days—so one night fell to her knees and prayed. *Dear Lord, let it come to me, let the text arrive as on a great four-masted schooner, let its pages flow from my hand as if from a grand river, let each chapter bind itself as if wrapped in reed, let the text be ancient but translated into my language with authentic fluidity, and I'll pay you for it, Lord, ten percent of my salary at the university I swear will be yours.*

Night after night, then, she dreamed of a certain river from her childhood, dreamed that she'd stolen a thesis, each page of it retrieved from the river as she waded in, each hung on a clothesline to dry. Day after day she transcribed it, and in June stood in defense of it, was brilliant, fluent with words she didn't know she knew.

You should publish this, her committee said—*this will be a classic.*

The composer said that birdsong was "God's language,"

and for the first time in half a century this was a god I might believe in. What if it was true, I thought, what if this god so remote, light years away in some palace whose architecture, elaborate, soaring, beyond the scope of our reckoning, turns out to be a god who speaks to us only in one voice: not the voice of proselytizer in the pulpit, but in simple birdsong. *Simple birdsong*, I heard myself think, then realized my error in that.

Hermit thrush, Wilson's warbler, veery, golden-crowned sparrow, who hasn't heard such a song then lapsed into silence, lacking not just the semantics but the mechanics of response?

Birds singing for days outside my mother's bedroom window as she lay dying.

This Water

The poet is in the center of a city known for its beauty. He's in a chair next to a circular fountain, the water of the fountain tinged green with algae, and in the center of the fountain a circle of eighteen jets, the jets on a timer, the water rising, falling, green-white against the clear blue sky.

He's reading poetry—a poet he loves from the High North. He reads the words but can't bring himself to concentrate. Though the man whose words he reads is long dead, the poet thinks of him as a friend, and when he travels in the city, the man's book in his briefcase—or, as now, in his hand—he feels that he has a friend with him.

Today, though, by the fountain, he reads the words *Now May is at the window* over and over, but finds himself losing interest, pulled away each time by the sound of the fountain, the height of its jets, and he sees now, knows now, that though long ago he consciously chose not to compete with other poets, every poet competes with water.

The Weeping Man, Paris

Tuesday afternoon she'd passed a man lying face down on the sidewalk in front of the *Hermes* store, clean powder-blue sweat pants, matching sweatshirt unstained.

The man was huge: at least three hundred pounds. It was late fall, the weather oddly warm, and before she saw the man she'd exulted at the clouds—saffron-tinged in late sun, quickly moving south, not a threat of rain in them, their shapes the fantastic figures children conjure.

The man was weeping inconsolably, his forehead on the pavement at the base of the marble *Hermes* steps, his right hand pounding the pavement, his body wracked in the sobbing, one hip raised, the word *Maman* cried over and over, but this man was no infant—he must have been fifty.

That night she slept poorly, dreamed of him, and Wednesday, unable to rest, exhausted, she felt debilitated. She'd hurried past that scene the day before, stopping only briefly—mere seconds—but in her dream, pausing beside her, stood a kind man, his eyes grieving for the weeping figure on the sidewalk, and, like her, frozen—unable to act.

Again Wednesday night she dreamed the scene, almost unchanged, then Thursday, and for that third night in a row she could find no relief: the sight of the man's back heaving, his voice, the man beside her in the dream looking into her eyes, wordless, helpless.

She knew that if her husband were alive he'd say *Stop it. Decide to stop it before you go to sleep and just stop it. You have the power to do that.* But her husband's heart had betrayed him, attacked him, and by Saturday she came to wonder who really she was dreaming of—she despised the weeping man, he disgusted her with his endless *Maman*s, his pitiful fat-fisted pounding,

Get up, you bastard, she screamed in her sleep, *Get up.*

Notes to the Reader

Some years ago, while editing *The Collected Poetry and Prose of Lawrence Fixel,* I became acquainted with David Miller, the English prose poet living in London. Miller and Fixel were friends, and as a result of our own correspondence and ensuing friendship Miller sent me his *Spiritual Letters,* * a thin volume of prose poems. The work in that book is neither *spiritual* in the strictly religious sense nor *letters* in the epistolary sense. Its spirituality—for me, at least, is one of an abiding, pulsing intelligence—and its *letters* essentially a nod to the literary.

These Miller prose poems were not of the kind to which I am usually drawn. They run a narrative line for a while, then abruptly flip to another strand of narrative, then perhaps back to the first, perhaps not: synaptical in that way. Here's an example:

> Sitting at a small table on the balcony, drinking wine and writing draft after draft by lamplight. More and more incapacitated, his head snapping backwards in spite of himself, the boy was stranded in the waiting room. Having dropped the heap of leaves, the little girl beseeched her sister and parents to help her pick them up again. You should try writing a novel, he told me. *Dear is the honie that is likt out of thornes.*

In some books of this kind, I give up quickly, finding them solipsistic, my remaining time on Earth not well spent puzzling them out.

In Miller's case, though, I found that those narrative leaps opened me in a new way, and found that by the time I was into the book a dozen pages, in a state of not-unhappy disorientation, certain small phrases triggered progressions of thought for me—often completely unrelated—and I followed.

I wrote a few pieces based on such phrases from Miller and soon came internally to call these The Miller Poems.

Before long I found that I had quite a few, and decided to make a discipline of it: I would read (no: *apprehend,* really) a page of these Spiritual Letters and seize on a phrase that jumped out—sometimes just a word or two, sometimes a longer run—and begin a new piece integrating, often deep inside the poem, those extracted words.

These "triggers" did not have the sense of "writing prompts," which I tend to mistrust in poetry as being extrinsic vs. intrinsic; instead, they had more the feel of having been engendered by a particular detail of a painting or a skew on a Biblical story, the new prose straying far from its source.

Over a period of a few years, then, along with my other writing, I'd regularly dip into the Miller book, write a piece, go on.

Ultimately there were perhaps a hundred, some respectable, some less, most still containing the original elemental triggering phrase, some having had those source words edited out in service of the poem.

The ones I considered respectable comprise this book.

For readers who might be interested, I list below the poems and "trigger phrases" that engendered them.

—Gerald Fleming
2021

TITLE	PHRASE
At the Lighthouse	*saw her turn over in sleep; the ruins of the old lighthouse*
Blue Iris	*blue iris; your poor daughter has died*
Brocade Dress	*brocade dress draped; a chair*
Chapel	*neglected*
Club	*He told the woman about the suicide attempt*
Collector of Titles	*I dream of him lending me books*
Fisherman	*"an amateur"; "I write, rewrite"*
Get him out of the wind	*Facing the wall, away from the wind*
Grand Design	*children's hospital*
He was the kind of man…	*listened to; stories*
In Recall	*memories, dreams*
In Silence	*a diamond setter*
In the cemetery we're between worlds…	*scribbled in the margins of the text,*
Lookout	*Yearning for an old friend*
My Andalusian Friend	*clarinet*

TITLE	PHRASE
Name Day	*meaningless din, sinking into despondency*
Night Scholar	*stolen; thesis; each page; retrieved from the river*
Nurse	*agony in the garden*
Outside Las Cruces	*the scrub ablaze*
Over There	*clean; clad*
Passage	*a chair strapped to her back*
Persephone off the Runway	*glass of water*
Progression	*locked out of his flat*
Second Door	*dwarfed by; shanty dwellings*
Shot	*unable to*
Sister, they called him	*Sister*
The Bastard and the Bishop	*a script, cryptic, enigmatic*
The Black Book	*The sheets of paper blacken*
The Collagist	*erasure and reversal*
The composer said that birdsong…	*The composer said that birdsong was "God's language"*
The fire two hundred miles away	*the lake, the trees illumined*
The Jokers	*two roosters; perched*
The Nightshift Brickmakers	*full moon; trees; long window*
The Old Books	*old poet*
The Sentimentalist	*I see young people on Bourke Street playing and think of you*
The tunnel foreman	*what he'd gone through*
The Weeping Man, Paris	*unable to rest; to act*
This Water	*losing interest*
To My Friend Bill, in the Ethers	*Lines from your writing*
To view the fireworks, then	*exploding lights; toward me*
Winter Coat	*the cat, shut inside one of your trunks*

*David Miller, *Spiritual Letters*, Chax Press, Tucson, Arizona, 2011.
(n.b.: A subsequent, expanded version of Miller's *Spiritual Letters* was published in London, 2017, by Contraband Press.)